Endorseme

"Christians are pressed by very real questions. How does Scripture structure a church, order worship, organize ministry, and define biblical leadership? Those are just examples of the questions that are answered clearly, carefully, and winsomely in this new series from 9Marks. I am so thankful for this ministry and for its incredibly healthy and hopeful influence in so many faithful churches. I eagerly commend this series."

R. Albert Mohler Jr., President, The Southern Baptist Theological Seminary

"Sincere questions deserve thoughtful answers. If you're not sure where to start in answering these questions, let this series serve as a diving board into the pool. These minibooks are winsomely to-the-point and great to read together with one friend or one hundred friends."

Gloria Furman, author, *Missional Motherhood* and *The Pastor's Wife*

"As a pastor, I get asked lots of questions. I'm approached by unbelievers seeking to understand the gospel, new believers unsure about next steps, and maturing believers wanting help answering questions from their Christian family, friends, neighbors, or coworkers. It's in these moments that I wish I had a book to give them that was brief, answered their questions, and pointed them in the right direction for further study. Church Questions is a series that provides just that. Each booklet tackles one question in a biblical, brief, and practical manner. The series may be called Church Questions, but it could be called 'Church Answers.' I intend to pick these up by the dozens and give them away regularly. You should too."

Juan R. Sanchez, Senior Pastor, High Pointe Baptist Church, Austin, Texas

"Where can we Christians find reliable answers to our common questions about life together at church—without having to plow through long, expensive books? The Church Questions booklets meet our need with answers that are biblical, thoughtful, and practical. For pastors, this series will prove a trustworthy resource for guiding church members toward deeper wisdom and stronger unity."

Ray Ortlund, President, Renewal Ministries

What Should
I Look For in
a Church?

Church Questions

What Should I Look For in a Church?

Alex Duke

CROSSWAY®

WHEATON, ILLINOIS

Trade paperback ISBN: 978-1-4335-7904-2
ePub ISBN: 978-1-4335-7907-3
PDF ISBN: 978-1-4335-7905-9
Mobipocket ISBN: 978-1-4335-7906-6

Library of Congress Cataloging-in-Publication Data

Names: Duke, Alex, author.
Title: What should I look for in a church? / Alex Duke.
Description: Wheaton, Il : Crossway, 2022. | Series: Church questions | Includes bibliographical references and index.
Identifiers: LCCN 2022011800 (print) | LCCN 2022011801 (ebook) | ISBN 9781433579042 (trade paperback) | ISBN 9781433579059 (pdf) | ISBN 9781433579066 (mobipocket) | ISBN 9781433579073 (epub)
Subjects: LCSH: Church. | Choice of church.
Classification: LCO BV600.3 .D85 2022 (print) | LCC BV600.3 (ebook) | DDC 262.001/7—dc23/eng/20220413
LC record available at https://lccn.loc.gov/2022011800
LC ebook record available at https://lccn.loc.gov/2022011801

Crossway is a publishing ministry of Good News Publishers.

BP		31	30	29	28	27	26	25	24	23	22
15	14	13	12	11	10	9	8	7	6	5	4	3	2	1

After this many of his disciples turned back and no longer walked with him. So Jesus said to the twelve, "Do you want to go away as well?" Simon Peter answered him, "Lord, to whom shall we go? You have the words of eternal life, and we have believed, and have come to know, that you are the Holy One of God."

John 6:66–69

The first church I can remember was Expressway Church of Christ. They chose the name, I assume, because it was a church of Christ right next to an expressway.

I remember two things about the preacher: his name (Greg) and his caterpillar mustache. I remember three things about this church:

- The pew Bibles turned Jesus's words red. One page was all red. As a child, I believed this had to be the best page in all the Bible.
- The Lord's Supper happened every week. And if you missed it in the morning, you had to

9

stand up during the evening service to get what you missed.

- The mustachioed preacher named Greg ended every sermon the same way, with an invitation "to rise up out of that watery grave, a new creation, born again."

One way or another, my parents' divorce led to our departure from the church by the expressway. The details were fuzzy then and remain fuzzy now. At ten-years-old, I was either not privy to them or my elementary-school mind crowded them out in favor of stats about Major League Baseball and Pokémon cards.

We ended up at a megachurch—and when I say "mega" I mean mega. Attendees in the tens of thousands. My old church had a "sanctuary"; this place had a "worship center." My old church had a few hallways; this place had a few escalators. My old church had pews; this place had individual seats, like an arena, only the "cup" holders were fit for communion juice, not $10 Miller Lites. My old church had flannelgraph boards in the kid's classroom; this place had GameCubes and a gym with a basketball court—actually, four basketball courts. I don't remember much about my early days here, except that everything seemed jaw-dropping and spectacular. I felt like I'd risen out of a watery grave and into a game room of wonders.

As a child, I believed this had to be the best place in all the world. Imagine getting your milk from a cow who's lived in your backyard all your life. Let's call her Bessy. Now imagine that Bessy dies or gets swept up in a tornado or whatever and, suddenly, you have to buy your milk at a Walmart. But not just any Walmart, one of those Walmart SuperCenters that absorb several city blocks and attract eccentrics en masse. You might miss your long-lost bovine buddy, but if you're honest, you'll also be kind of mesmerized by this new land flowing with milk and Honey Nut Cheerios.

That's basically how I felt. The stark differences between church #1 and church #2 were more overwhelming than they were legible. It's like describing the difference between noon and midnight. Over the next eight years—from age ten to eighteen, when I went off to college—this megachurch, though it looked like a mansion, became my home. God saved me under its faithful ministry. What stands out to me now, more than two decades later, is not its fantastic features but the faces of faithful men who pushed me to love and follow Jesus: Jonathan, Bobby, Rick, Matt, Dave, and others.[1]

I'm thankful for that church.

If we had more time, I could tell you about the church I joined my freshman year of college where—on Super Bowl Sunday 2008—the pastors dressed up as Tom Brady and Eli Manning. I could tell you about how their seats had real cup-holders, not for Miller Lites but for the complementary Cokes you could get in the lobby.

Or I could tell you about the church I went to for most of my college years. The nondescript one that sat between a field and another field. It was led by Pastor Steve and his perpetually gray five-o'clock shadow. It's where I learned about the beauty of the Bible and the majesty of God's grace to sinners like me.[2]

Or I could tell you about the church I went to during seminary, where the pastor explained that he was a "Calminian."[3] It endured a church split that eventually became a church plant called, without even the slightest sense of irony, Unity Community Church.[4] This church wasn't without its struggles, but it was—and is!—full of wonderful and godly people.

Or I could tell you about the first church I worked at in Queens, NY, with Vinny Nizzo— a deacon who looks and talks like a wise guy from *Goodfellas*. Vinny didn't become a Christian until later in life, and he now writes poetry every morning and sends his edifying poems to hundreds of people every day before dawn.[5]

Or I could tell you about the church I work at now, nestled next to a big university and teeming with young families. It employs me to, somewhat bizarrely, teach the youth group and lead something called an "Ecclesiology Seminar."

That's the broad sweep of my church history. I could tell you more about each, but as I reflect even now on these churches, I'm filled with gratitude. No church was perfect, but each has played a significant role in helping me to think about what makes a healthy and helpful church.

9Marks, Taco Bell, Expositional Preaching, and a Cheesy Gordita Crunch

Of course, the goal of this booklet isn't to tell you about my church past, but to help you with your church future. I want to help you answer the question: "What should I look for in a church?" I've heard lots of good answers to that question. I've spent nearly the past decade working for a ministry called 9Marks whose sole mission is basically to help people answer that question.

My boss likes to say that 9Marks is like a Mexican restaurant. We use the same ingredients, but we just present them differently. Our meat, cheese, beans, and rice are expositional preaching, biblical theology, the gospel, conversion, evangelism, church membership, church discipline, elders, discipling, missions, and prayer. Our delivery mechanism—our tortillas and our gorditas, our chips and our sopas—may change, but the message remains more or less the same.

So let me cut to the quick. What should you look for in a church?

1. Look for a Church That Knows You're Gonna Die

I recently watched Alfred Hitchcock's classic film *North by Northwest*. Every actor in that film is either dead or nearly dead. Cary Grant? Dead, for a while now. Martin Landeau? Dead, only recently. Eva Marie Saint? As of this writing, she's ninety-seven. I wonder if she'll be alive by the time these words move from my computer screen to your eyes on actual pages. Back in 1959, they looked so timelessly vibrant, so unquenchably full of life. Now they are all dead or knocking on death's door.

I suppose I should just get right to it. You're gonna die. Your light will be snuffed out. The Grim Reaper will come calling. Your time will come. You'll kick the bucket. You'll give up the ghost. You'll "depart" from this life. We love to cloak our fears in euphemisms, don't we? But whatever you want to call it, you and I and everyone you have ever known and everyone you will ever know will die (unless Jesus returns).

If you had a broken arm, you'd go to a doctor, and he would fix it. If you want to set your family up for a secure financial future, you'd go to a financial advisor, and he would help.

But what should we do about *this* problem of death? What should we do about our shared and inevitable future demise? Where do we go for help? We can go to a doctor to "delay" this future or an investment banker to prep for this future or a Maserati dealer to numb us to the inevitability of this future. But these places can't give us anything we can take with us to "the other side." We need something mothproof and rustproof. Where do we get that?

We *should* get that at our local church.

The Bible sometimes tells us what we already know: "It is appointed for man to die once" (Heb. 9:27). Now, what I've just done here is reference a verse to make a point while ignoring its meaning in context.

But those words don't just show up out of nowhere, like Kramer at Jerry's door. They're part of a larger argument. Let me give you a bit more context. Here are the verses just before Hebrews 9:27:

> For Christ has entered, not into holy places made with hands, which are copies of the true things, but into heaven itself, now to appear in the presence of God on our behalf. Nor was it to offer himself repeatedly, as the high priest enters the holy places every year with blood not his own, for then he would have had to suffer repeatedly since the foundation of the world. But as it is, he has appeared once for all at the end of the ages to put away sin by the sacrifice of himself. (Heb. 9:24–26)

Woah! We went from a commonsense, declarative sentence—basically, "You will die someday"[6]—to talking about Jesus appearing in heaven to offer himself as a sacrifice, similar to the high priest but also kind of different.

What's going on? How can we explain this labyrinth of logic? Let me try.

The author of Hebrews wants us to rejoice in the fact that Jesus's death improves on and therefore eliminates the need for any sacrificial system outside himself. So he's saying Jesus died and then waltzed right into his Father's presence. As far as it goes, this is precisely what the High Priest did when he entered the handmade tabernacle, which the author of Hebrews calls "copies of the true things" (v. 24).

Okay, so what did Jesus *do* when he got there? This is where his work differs from the high priest. He doesn't offer sacrifices "repeatedly" with "blood not his own," like the High Priest did (v. 25). The High Priest had to show up "with bells on"[7] and the blood of a bull every year for the Day of Atonement. Yet Jesus's sacrifice, was *different*. He didn't have to "suffer repeatedly" (v. 26) like Sisyphus or New York Mets fans. Why? Because when Jesus put away sin he didn't bring a proxy into a replica; he brought himself into the *real thing*, into heaven, into the unmediated, undiluted, unobstructed presence of God. And he did so for us (v. 24). *His blood* was the sacrifice for sin that cancels out the need for another.

Now back to our verses in question:

> And just as it is appointed for man to die once, and after that comes judgment, so Christ, having been offered once to bear the sins of many, will appear a second time, not to deal with sin but to save those who are eagerly waiting for him. (Heb. 9:27–28)

We see that our commonsense, declarative statement isn't the main point but rather an aside to make a point about Jesus. So we might restate Hebrews 9:27–28 like this: "Just like *your* death and judgment is certain, so too is Christ's second appearance during which he will finish what he started. Since he's already dealt with sin through his death, he now only has one job left for his people: to save them from judgment."

You're gonna die. And after that? You'll face judgment. Will Jesus face it for you? Or will you be left to fend for yourself?

Wait a second. You thought we were here to learn about what we should look for in a church! And now we're suddenly talking about death and eternal judgment? Let me explain: If this topic seems strange or overly severe to you, if you only hear about death in the abstract, clouded and dulled by euphemisms and allusions, if you never consider the certain concrete realities you will face *after* death—namely, a personalized judgment for your sins—then I suspect you don't go to a healthy church. I suspect that your pastor may not be helping you face your biggest, most inescapable problem.

I'm not recommending a so-called fire-and-brimstone preacher. I'm not saying every sermon should dwell on death and God's judgment. But I want to return to the questions I asked at the beginning: What should we do about our shared and inevitable future demise? Where should we go for help? We should go to the local church because it's *there* that we're comforted with and called to celebrate the only remedy for our unsolvable problem: the person and work of Jesus Christ. *Jesus* delivers us from our death, a death we earned because of our sin against the Lord. *Jesus* saves us from judgment, which we earned because of our sin against the Lord. So when I say "look for a church that knows you're gonna die," I am *also saying* "look for a church that speaks about sin and its consequences with clarity and compassion." Look for a church that knows we cannot fix our sin problem with mere moral improvement or ideological assent or theological aptitude or emotional forthrightness. We need Christ.

Our world is chock-full of problems. But the Lord has given the local church a particular and peculiar message, and it ought to remain our focus. Because if *we* stop holding up Christ crucified and risen for sinners, then who else will take our place?

Here's a challenge for you. Pay close attention to how the preachers you listen to talk about sin.

I've heard some pastors talk about sin as if it's little more than the emotionally unhealthy labels we give ourselves: broken, unlovable, hopeless, etc. While these labels articulate some of the alienating *effects* of sin, while they appropriately explore our subjective experience of *being a sinner*, they both obscure sin's essence and undermine our agency and culpability before the Lord. If that's the primary way you think of sin, then you've adopted pop psychology more than biblical truth—more Dr. Phil than the Apostle Paul.

Of course, sin is something done *to* us—sadly, some have much more experience with this than others. But if we stop there, we've evacuated the Bible's teaching on the topic. Why? Because no one disagrees with this. Blame-shifting and finger-pointing come so easily to us. It's our natural, post-fall state: "The woman whom you gave to be with me, she gave me fruit of the tree, and I ate" (Gen. 3:12).

It doesn't require a work of God to convince people they're victims of others' sin. It also doesn't require a work of God to convince people they've been materially affected by others' sin. But it's quite difficult, certainly so apart from God's grace, to convince people that they themselves are high-handed perpetrators of sin against both God and others, that their decency deserves death.

So churches should speak about sin *primarily* (though not exclusively) as our personal and willful rebellion against God and not as a social and indirect label given to us by others or ourselves. They should be clear that Jesus died on the cross as a substitute for sinners, not as a rudder for the rudderless (Rom. 3:25; 1 John 2:2; 4:10).

I don't mean to deny the comprehensive nature of Christ's work—he does indeed restore the broken, love the unlovely, and give hope to the hopeless; yes, and amen!—but precisely none of that is accessible apart from Christ absorbing God's wrath for sinners, apart from swallowing our judgment by his death, apart from him providing the remedy for our most unavoidable problem: we're gonna die one day.[8]

Because not only will we all die, we will also all live forever. And when we die, we can take only one of two things with us into eternity: our sin or the salvation won for us by Jesus. If you possess the latter through faith in Christ, then you've finally got something that death can't take from you, that won't eventually become moth food. You have exactly what you need to persevere until your death. That is Peter's point at the beginning of his letters to Christians who are experiencing suffering:

> Blessed be the God and Father of our Lord Jesus Christ! According to his great mercy, he has caused us to be born again to a living hope through the resurrection of Jesus Christ from the dead, to an inheritance that is imperishable, undefiled, and unfading, kept in heaven for you, who by God's power are being guarded through faith for a salvation ready to be revealed in the last time. In this you rejoice, though now for a little while, if necessary, you have been grieved by various trials, so that the tested genuineness of your faith—more precious than gold that perishes though it is tested by fire—may be found to result in praise and glory and honor at the revelation of Jesus Christ. Though you have not

seen him, you love him. Though you do not now see him, you believe in him and rejoice with joy that is inexpressible and filled with glory, obtaining the outcome of your faith, the salvation of your souls. (1 Pet. 1:3–9)

Look for a church that doesn't merely *acknowledge* sin and salvation and eternity but one where those truths shape its ministry and clarify its priorities. Non-Christians need this message, first and foremost. But Christians need it too!

Specific questions to ask:

- Does the church clearly explain the reality of our sin, the necessity of Jesus's death and resurrection, and the obligation we have to turn from our sin and trust in Jesus?
- Does the church clearly discuss the certainty of God's judgment against sin and the eternal hope we have in heaven because of Jesus?
- Does the preacher do all this . . . every single time he preaches?

2. Look for a Church Where the Bible Isn't Just for the Super-Serious, Super-Christians but for Everyone

I recently had a conversation with a Christian I have a lot of respect for. He's taught Bible classes and Sunday schools. Somehow, the topic of conversation got around to what happens when someone dies without ever hearing the gospel or even the name of Jesus. I simply *assumed* he would agree with me that conscious, personal faith in Jesus is a prerequisite for salvation. So you can imagine my surprise when *he* was surprised when I affirmed that such people will go to hell.

"I just don't understand how that would be," he said. "They believed based on what they could know." I pointed him to a few verses, but he couldn't shake his instinctual precommitment to what theology textbooks call *inclusivism*, which is just a fancy word for "there's a way to get to heaven through Jesus without specifically believing in Jesus."

How could this be? How could his theological instincts be so . . . off? When I asked him to defend what he believed from Scripture, he couldn't, which bothered me more than it seemed to bother him. What happened here? In short, I'm convinced my friend is like a lot of Christians. Many Christians' intuitions aren't shaped by the Bible because their churches rarely confront their people's intuitions *with* the Bible.

I've been taught that preachers should assume their audience is both very intelligent and very uneducated. That seems right to me. So many churches are full of saints who are full of the Spirit but empty on Scripture. Of course, they know the coffee-mug and above-the-sink verses. They know Jesus fed five thousand folks with fish and bread. They know Genesis is at the beginning and Revelation[9] is at the end, and they know the broad outline in-between with Adam and Noah and Abraham and Moses and David and all the rest.

But there's a ton of stuff they *don't* know that, frankly, they should know. They probably couldn't explain the theological reasoning behind the tabernacle and the sacrificial system apart from "that's just the way God wanted it." They couldn't tell you what's happening in Isaiah or Jeremiah. They couldn't recognize departures from the Trinity or defend the deity of Christ or explain the necessity of a historical Adam.[10]

Stray verses fill your average saint with joy and vigor, but whole books vex and bewilder them. The Bible is as enlightening and encouraging as it is inscrutable and unwieldy. And so, sadly, many Christians simply shrug their shoulders and stick to what they know, to their favorite parts, or to what seems most applicable to them in the moment.

Look back a few pages to those verses in Hebrews 9. My guess is that most church-going Christians wouldn't be able to read them and tell you what they mean. Why? Well, it's certainly *not* because they're dumb—and it's not because they lack desire. They couldn't do it for the same reason I can't do a pull-up. They've not strengthened the right muscles.

And here's the saddest part about all of this: their churches offer little help. Well, that's not entirely true. Almost every church offers Sunday schools and Bible studies and d-groups and book clubs that cover all that I've mentioned and more! But they're offered as ancillary exercises, optional exits off the main highway. They're not the entrees but the desserts or appetizers. The main meal—by which I mean the sermon during the Sunday gathering, the thing that most Christians feel conscience-bound to attend—simply fails to raise Christians' biblical and theological IQ. It fails to put ballast in the boat. And the result? Saints are tossed to and fro (Eph. 4:14).

But here's what's jarring. This failure is rarely due to incompetence or boring preaching or actively bad false teaching.[11] The failure is *on purpose*. Why? Because for many churches, Sundays intentionally aim at a different target. They're for bringing your non-Christian friends to hear about how Jesus can help make sense of their messed-up lives. (Which is good!) Or they're for parsing out bite-sized biblical truths so that Christians will have clarity on how to be a better _____ or how to stop _____ or how to understand how _____ interacts with _____. I'm not trying to play Mad Libz, but however your subconscious fills in those blanks likely hits the nail on the head better than anything I could write.[12]

So . . . look for a church where the Bible isn't for super-serious super-Christians, where you don't have to "opt in" to serious study of it. Look for a church where the Bible isn't sidelined to Sunday school or other sub-groups. Look for a church that isn't trying to feed you topical tapas but a five-course meal.

What does that look like? It looks like your pastor preaching through entire books of the Bible. It looks like sermons whose messages are predetermined by what passage comes next.[13] It looks like a church where the preacher doesn't imply there's ambiguity in the Bible on contested topics like sexuality and gender. The regular diet of every church should be God's word explained and applied—both to believers for their edification and encouragement and to unbelievers for their conviction and conversion.

Many other priorities will *seem* more urgent and more promising. Pastors and churches will be tempted to "go away" in search of something else that more obviously "works." In these moments, we need to remember what Peter said to Jesus when he faced a similar temptation: "Lord, to whom shall we go? You have the words of eternal life" (John 6:68).

Specific questions to ask:

- Do the preachers at this church walk through books of the Bible in their sermons?
- Do they seek to explain *and apply* God's word?
- Who are the sermons "pitched" to? Believers or nonbelievers? Saints or "seekers"?
- Do members seem more attached to their small group or to a specific ministry they're involved in?

3. Look for a Church That's More Than a Preaching Station

I love expositional preaching. It re-centered my ideological world, exploded my love for Jesus, and opened my mind to the wonders of the Scriptures. But expositional preaching has never loved me back.

Do you know what *has* loved me back? Burritos. I'm just kidding! *People* have loved me back.

Just yesterday, my wife and I moved for the tenth time in nine years. Do you know who showed up? Lots of people who loved me: my dad, my step-mom, my best friend of twenty years, and a girl from youth group who kept an eye on the little ones. But the vast majority of folks who showed up were members from my church. They love me too, even though some don't know me well. There was Bill, a fiftysomething truck driver who offered to drive the rental truck and save me from committing vehicular manslaughter. There was Joseph, a carpenter (no, not *that* Joseph the carpenter) who stayed until after dark to fix a few rickety cabinets. There was Ethan, a college student and new Christian who brought along a few guys he's discipling. There was Trent, an aggie with a pickup and who probably sleeps in his cowboy boots. Some of these folks I know quite well, but many I didn't know at all. I even had to ask a few folks their names!

What should you look for in a church? You should look for a church full of people who love you not because they're related to you and not because of your decades-long shared history and not because of your kindred political preferences. Look for a church full of people who love you because *of course they do*. Because of course a hand loves a foot, and an eye loves an ear. As members of the same church, any precondition for love has already been met simply by being a part of the same body.

When you hear the word "church," what comes to mind? Probably a building. Maybe the inside of one—maybe red carpets and beige walls. Maybe the outside of one—a brick building topped with a cross. That's fine. But biblically speaking, a church is more of a people than a place. Or, better, a church is *a people* who have been redeemed by the same Lord, who are now therefore *reconciled* to one another, and who regularly gather together.

If you've spent any time reading the news or on social media over the past few years, it's clear that one mark of the world is tribalism.

Tribalism is just a fancy theological word for saying that we tend to be suspicious of folks who aren't like us. As a result, we divide them up according to various group identities and then assign undesirable traits to them or assume undesirable things about them. Our tribalism enables us to arrive at unconscious assessments of people. In more severe situations, these unconscious assessments may encourage us to rationalize others' mistreatment, or to believe we are somehow more intrinsically valuable or righteous than those who aren't like us.

I bet you have various "tribes" in your mind even as you're reading this. You know who the white hats and black hats are; you've seen them on Facebook or other social media sites. And yet, if by some strange stroke of God's providence and marketing miracle, the person next to you were reading these exact paragraphs, I suspect they would *also* have tribes in their minds—except the hats would be switched, the roles reversed.

Like *Beauty and the Beast*, tribalism is a tale as old as time. We divvy ourselves up according to ethnicity, gender identity, sexual orientation, religious status, economic class, political party, favorite sports team, or preferred comic book brand. So whether we're talking about the Hutus and Tutsis in Rwanda, the Brahmans and the Untouchables in India, the Protestants and the Catholics in Northern Ireland, or the welfare recipients in the city and those born with a silver-spoon in the suburbs—these instincts to divide run deep. They're both serious (untold lives have been lost due to tribal conflicts) and silly (who cares if you like Marvel or DC?).

Christianity takes a wrecking ball to all of this. I don't mean to imply that Christianity teaches us that these various identities don't exist. Of course they do. And each comes with its accompanying set of blessings and burdens. But I do mean to say that Christianity urges us to consider and live according to our essential *similarities* more than it urges us to define ourselves by our occasional *differences*, and it turns those differences into blessings, as each part of the body brings a particular benefit to the whole.

The best unredeemed humanity can do is foster temporary unity around transient causes.

Honestly, the best it can do is a football game, when we're all in the stadium together, and nothing else matters expect beating our common enemy—in my case, the University of Kentucky Wildcats and the referees I've convinced myself they've paid. We're all cheering and booing at the right times. We're high-fiving and hugging and feverishly analyzing the state of play with our neighbors and newfound friends. Not a sports fan? Okay, I'll switch the metaphor. The best the world can offer is a concert, when we're all there together, singing the same tune at the top of our lungs, and nothing else matters except the next beloved line. But after the whistle blows or the encore ends, what happens? We disperse. Our temporary unity recedes. Our in-sync chants fade as everyone begins to sing their own tune. Our common enemy disappears, our common goal stands in the rearview mirror, and so we go our own ways—emotionally spent but ultimately unchanged.

But here's what Jesus does in the local church. He takes the chants of diverse and even divided people and unites them in an unbreakable unity for an eternal mission. He stoops down and scoops up the shards of our divvied-up identities and he makes us whole—*together*. After describing how each of us came to Christ *individually* (Eph. 2:1–10), Paul then describes what Christ is building *corporately*:

Therefore remember that at one time you Gentiles in the flesh, called "the uncircumcision" by what is called the circumcision, which is made in the flesh by hands— remember that you were at that time separated from Christ, alienated from the commonwealth of Israel and strangers to the covenants of promise, having no hope and without God in the world. But now in Christ Jesus you who once were far off have been brought near by the blood of Christ. For he himself is our peace, who has made us both one and has broken down in his flesh the dividing wall of hostility by abolishing the law of commandments expressed in ordinances, that he might create in himself one new man in place of the two, so making peace, and might reconcile us both to God in one body through the cross, thereby killing the hostility. And he came and preached peace to you who were far off and peace to those who were near. For through him we both have access in one Spirit to the Father. So then you are no longer strangers and aliens, but you are fellow citizens with the saints and members of the household of God, built on the foundation of the apostles and prophets, Christ Jesus himself being the cornerstone, in whom the whole structure, being joined together, grows into a holy temple in the Lord. In him you also are being built together into a dwelling place for God by the Spirit. (Eph. 2:11–22)

If we're Christians, then all of that is *objectively* and *perfectly* true of us because Christ has done it for us. But that doesn't mean we just sit back and relax. It means we get to work. After all, our *objective* and *perfect* realities now place claims on our lives. It's like marriage. When you say "I do" and kiss your spouse, you are objectively and perfectly married. Your marriage is *done*. But your work at being married—at being a husband and a wife—is only just beginning. Your marriage has ushered you into a new relationship with new claims and expectations both to God and to others that will shape your life until death do you part. Because though you are perfectly married, you are *not* the perfect spouse.

That's why Paul follows up his declaration about what Christ has done with what we must do. He even links the two explicitly:

> I therefore, a prisoner for the Lord, urge you to walk in a manner worthy of the calling to which you have been called, with all humility and gentleness, with patience, bearing with one another in love, eager to maintain the unity of the Spirit in the bond of peace. There is one body and one Spirit—just as you were called to the one hope that belongs to your call—one Lord, one faith, one baptism, one God and Father of all, who is over all and through all and in all. (Eph. 4:1–6)

Okay, so what? What do we actually *do* to "walk in a worthy manner"? In other words, what do humility and gentleness and patience and love and unity *look like*? Great questions. Maybe something like this.

You speak truthfully to one another—even when it's hard. After all, you're members of the same family. You're as close as close can get. When a fellow Christian sins against you, you resist sinful anger. And when anger bubbles up, you work hard to confess it and move forward because you know unconfessed anger is an opportunity for the devil to wreak havoc and wreck unity. You use your job as a platform not for self-promotion, but for generosity, to look out for those in need so that you might help them. You use your words carefully, not like acid but like aloe vera. They don't corrode and condemn; they soothe and heal. You remember how the Holy Spirit has worked identically in every fellow Christian, and so you await an identical future. You're more alike than you realize, so you work hard to assume the best and to see other saints how Christ sees them—even when you want to respond in bitterness, frustration, and even malice. After all, you once faced a debt you could never repay, even if you had all the resources and all the time in the universe. But God in Christ forgave you. On your best days, his generosity and kindness motivate yours. On your worst days, his generosity and kindness are shared with you anyway. Hallelujah, what a Savior.

What you just read is how the Bible describes holiness with its boots on the ground (Eph. 4:25–31). It's how the Bible describes a church. I don't mean the *ideal* church, you know, like one that could only exist in make-believe lands like Narnia. I mean the biblical church, like one that exists in normal places like Nebraska.

Let's remember what we're doing. We're talking about what you should look for in a church. I'm trying to tell you that you should look for a church that's not just a preaching station. What do I mean? I mean that when you're committing to a church, you're not committing to your favorite Sunday-morning preacher. You're not committing to whatever music or mission or vibe you appreciate most. You're not even most fundamentally committing to a theological persuasion, though theology is certainly important. No, when you commit to a church, you're most fundamentally committing to *people*, people like Bill and Joseph and Atito and Chelsea and Jonathan and Jason and Morgan. They love you. You love them. They help you move. You help them move. They make you mad. You make them mad. They forgive. You forgive. And on and on and on it goes.

A church isn't a crowd of Christians who show up at the same time every week for some music and a message. A church is a *people* who have committed themselves to help each other get to heaven.[14]

Every church, of course, promises "authentic" or "deep" relationships. But these stated goals often run against the grain of what they actually do and the kinds of relationships they prioritize. So let me be clear: you should look for a church that practices meaningful membership and discipline. In a church where "community" is highlighted but there's no meaningful practice of membership, it's easy to slip in and out unnoticed and therefore hard to know who's following Christ and who's just there out of convenience. In a church where "community" is highlighted but there's no meaningful practice of discipline, it's easy to lead a double life and therefore hard to believe that anyone is taking this whole thing *that* seriously. Don't get me wrong: some relationships may be genuine and even genuinely deep, but they are at the end of the day functionally opt-in and self-determined.[15]

A few weeks ago, I had a conversation with someone who was leaving her church. The church hadn't met her expectations. Friendships weren't forming, and so she and her husband were out. Their church had become a preaching station to them. "All we have is the preaching," she said.[16]

I'm glad she knew that preaching doesn't make a church. While it should facilitate the relationships in the church, it can never become a substitute for them. Why? Because preaching doesn't love you back. It can't. But people will. And if you commit yourself to them—and allow them to commit themselves to you, even to the point of inconvenience and sacrifice—then over time those relationships will flourish.

Specific questions to ask:

- Does this church have a meaningful membership process?
- Does the church have regular members' meetings?
- Does the church practice church discipline when a member persists in serious, unrepentant sin?
- Are organic discipling relationships normal? Or is growth and accountability outsourced to programs and/or staff?

Let's see if I can summarize what I've written so far in three pieces of advice.

1. Look for a church that preaches the gospel clearly, so clearly that you are not confused as to what your problem is and what God's solution is in Christ.
2. Look for a church where God's word is placed on a pedestal for all, not a conveyor belt for the curious.

3. Look for a church that ushers you into a community of supernatural relationships, which sounds weird but is just normal Christians pursuing holiness together.

If you find a church like that, then I'm confident you'll find a wonderful place, somewhere worth settling down for a while, perhaps even for the rest of your life. The gospel, the Bible, and meaningful relationships are the most important. They should be at the top of your list. You should care about other stuff too: qualified leaders, clarity on difficult doctrines, clarity on ethical issues like sexuality and abortion. I could keep going. After all, this book isn't exhaustive, I'm just giving you the basics.

But . . . I've only got a few hundred words left in my word count, so let me throw out one more piece of counsel for you to chew on.

4. Don't Look for Perfection

I told you a little bit about my church history at the beginning. If I could summarize it into a sentence: Over time, God's word clarified all sorts of back-of-my-head questions that I didn't know how to articulate.

- Why did it always strike me as a bit odd that some of my friends' parents were "members" of the church that they never seemed to go to?
- Why did I find it weird, even as an eighteen-year-old, that my church devoted a Sunday to the Super Bowl?
- Why did I grow so much when I finally arrived at a church that simply explained and applied the Bible?
- Why did it seem weird that some churches had "services" like a movie theater had "showtimes"? Or "sites" like a fast-food location had "franchises"?

These were questions I didn't know I had until I knew I had them, until the opposite of the practice I'd always known had been plopped in front of my face.

I hope to have given you some ability to articulate the kinds of questions you should be asking when you are looking for a church. Because more than anything, I want you to *find* a healthy church. I'm not sure there's anything more important.

If I could be so bold: The goal of this little booklet is so that you'll be like me, a guy who found what he needed in the church even though he didn't go looking for it. I basically bumped into a healthy church. I want you to seek after one with everything you have. And when you find one, I want you to drink it in, like a thirsty man chugs a tall glass of ice-cold water. I want you to find a church that will stay with you when you leave—whether you've been there for a year, a decade, or a lifetime.

Here's another goal of this little booklet: don't be like me. You see, something terrible happened as I began to learn and believe this awesome stuff about the importance of the church: I became a jerk. In fact, I remember sitting down with my patient, longsuffering dad over some buffalo wings and giving him a talking-to, "The sermons at your church aren't even for Christians! Your preacher doesn't preach the gospel! Your 'sites' aren't even churches!"

Sin is the worst. It makes us stupid and stubborn when we're wrong, and it tempts us to become jerks when we're right and especially when we *think* we're right.

In short: don't be a jerk. Don't give the side-eye to other Christians and other churches. Assume the best. Look for churches that celebrate what they share in common with other true churches, and avoid churches that seem to revel in their uniqueness or innovation. Look for churches led by men with thick skin and tender hearts, who speak with compassion and clarity. Look for churches full of flourishing women—both married and single, wife and widow.

And always remember: no church is perfect. If you ever find one that is, you'll ruin it the moment you walk through the doors. So don't be like me, a jerk-in-recovery. Instead, be like Jesus. Find a church that helps you grow into maturity. As you do, give thanks to God for every church and every shepherd you've had along the way—as imperfect as they were.

Recommended Resources

Mark Dever, *Nine Marks of a Healthy Church*.
Wheaton, IL: Crossway, 2021.

Mark Dever, *What Is a Healthy Church?* Wheaton,
IL: Crossway, 2005.

Jonathan Leeman and Colin Hansen, *Rediscover
Church: Why the Body of Christ Is Essential*.
Wheaton, IL: Crossway, 2021.

Notes

1. Personal stories involving other individuals are shared in this booklet with permission. Sometimes pseudonyms have been used for privacy.

2. I love Pastor Steve. His preaching changed my life. I wrote an ode to him on 9Marks called "How I Accidentally Stumbled Across—And Then Fell in Love With—the Ordinary Means of Grace," 9Marks website, July 26, 2021, https://www.9marks.org/article/how-i-accidentally-stumbled-across-and-then-fell-in-love-with-the-ordinary-means-of-grace/.

3. For those without extraordinary deduction powers, "Calminian" is a portmanteau. Like, how Tiger Woods is Cablinasian. In other words, the pastor was trying to say that he was both a Calvinist *and* an Arminian.

4. Spoiler alert: Unity Community Church did not survive.

5. Today's poem was titled "The Tree," and it was sent at 6:02 a.m.

6. For a daily reminder of this, join 42,000+ people who follow @death_reminder on Twitter.

7. See Exodus 28:34–35, where it describes the bells on Aaron's robe. (He was the first high priest in Israel). I wonder if that's where the phrase "with bells on" came from.

8. The previous five paragraphs are adapted from an article I wrote called "You're So Depraved, You Probably Think This Church Is about You: How Total Depravity Upends Attractionalism," 9Marks website, February 5, 2019, https://www.9marks.org/article/youre-so -depraved-you-probably-think-this-church-is-about -you-how-total-depravity-upends-attractionalism/.

9. Though they might call it "Revelation*s*."

10. I'm not saying they ought to be able to describe to me the *extra Calvinisticum*. I simply mean that most Christians couldn't even explain the basics of these essential doctrines—and therefore probably can't identify a threat to them or a departure from them. If you want to be discouraged, check out Ligonier's 2020 Theology Survey at this link: https://thestate oftheology.com.

11. And to be honest, sometimes, the failure isn't on the church at all but entirely on the individual who is hooked up to an IV cocktail of Facebook, cable-news, and *Jesus Calling*.

12. It's not the goal of this little booklet to argue against the seeker-sensitive ministry model. But if you're interested in that argument, I make it in "You're So Depraved You Probably Think This Church Is about You."

13. It's not the goal of this little booklet to argue for what's called "expositional preaching." But you can read about the time I first encountered it in "How I Accidentally Stumbled Across—And Then Fell in Love With—The Ordinary Means of Grace."

14. Hat-tip to Mark Dever for this phrase.

15. For more on this topic, you could check out my previous installment in this series: *What Should We Do about Members Who Won't Attend?* (Crossway, 2021). I make the case for membership and discipline in that booklet. Here, I'm more-or-less assuming it.

16. Side-note: Someone *could* say, "All we have is the preaching" and mean, "All we have is the preaching and not the various programs and subgroups that we need to 'feel' connected." If that's the case, then I'd be less sympathetic. Faithful preaching should be at the center of a church's life, and the relationships will likely be downstream from it.

Scripture Index

IX 9Marks

Building Healthy Churches

9Marks exists to equip church leaders with a biblical vision and practical resources for displaying God's glory to the nations through healthy churches.

To that end, we want to see churches characterized by these nine marks of health:

1. Expositional Preaching
2. Gospel Doctrine
3. A Biblical Understanding of Conversion and Evangelism
4. Biblical Church Membership
5. Biblical Church Discipline
6. A Biblical Concern for Discipleship and Growth
7. Biblical Church Leadership
8. A Biblical Understanding of the Practice of Prayer
9. A Biblical Understanding and Practice of Missions

Find all our Crossway titles and other resources at 9Marks.org.

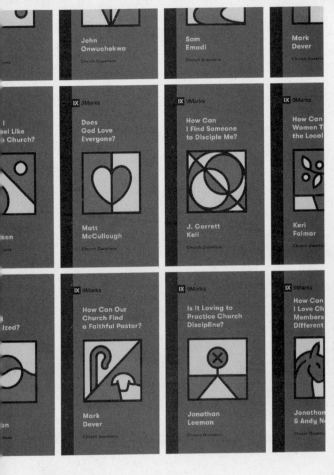

John
Onwuchekwa
Church Questions

Sam
Emadi
Church Questions

Mark
Dever
Church Questions

IX 9Marks

Does
God Love
Everyone?

Matt
McCullough
Church Questions

IX 9Marks

How Can
I Find Someone
to Disciple Me?

J. Garrett
Kell
Church Questions

IX 9Marks

How Can
Women T
the Local

Keri
Folmar
Church Questions

el Like
Church?

sen

IX 9Marks

How Can Our
Church Find
a Faithful Pastor?

Mark
Dever
Church Questions

IX 9Marks

Is It Loving to
Practice Church
Discipline?

Jonathan
Leeman
Church Questions

IX 9Marks

How Can
I Love Ch
Members
Different

Jonathan
& Andy N
Church Questions

ized?

on

IX 9Marks Church Questions

Providing ordinary Christians with sound and
accessible biblical teaching by answering
common questions about church life.

For more information, visit crossway.org.